STORIES THEY NEVER HEARD

Gregory John Ferris

This is a collection of stories from cousins who are descendants of Peter and Anna Dietz.

Many of the memories within this book are of the family farm in Kersey, Pennsylvania, where the importance of what was new was equaled by what was not.

Maintaining family ties can be difficult across generations, much less so with individual effort. I hope that more cousins, and their spouses, share stories of their own lives with each other, and in a way with our ancestors, in subsequent editions of this first attempt.

It is only because the world we know changes, that our memories are precious.

Gregg Ferris
May 2025

The cover photo, courtesy of Jane (Parmigiani) Huff is of Anna and Peter Dietz on their wedding day, September 20, 1904, aged 22 and 31 respectively. They are flanked by Anna's sister Barbara (Krellner) Kramer, and Peter's brother John Dietz.

The two photos on the rear cover were provided by Sandra (Parmigiani) Blomgren. The upper photograph, unfortunately blurry, is of Sandra (Sandy) and her brother John in the barn. Sandra was adamant on its inclusion.

The lower image is of Sandra with Dolly and foal Rowdy in the back pasture, near the small pond and old railroad grade. Dolly and Rowdy were equally insistent on this photo's inclusion.

Both photos are from the 1970s.

To keep the costs of production low, no interior photographs are included.

Stories appear in the order in which they were received while preparing this book.

Very limited edited was done, in order to preserve each contributor's distinct voice and style.

For Anna and Peter

Eva Long

Gregg's mother (Gertrude Dietz) and my mother (Alice Brown Dietz) were best friends. It was she who introduced my mother to my dad (Philip Dietz).

There was a part of Kersey that my mother called Irish Town. I'm not sure which part. I remember in the middle of Kersey there was a grocery store and a post office in the same building. One side was the grocery store, and the other side was the post office. Across the street, a road led to the house where we lived. To get there we had to go by a swamp. Now for my story

When I was a child, we used to have campfires, and the grown-ups would tell ghost stories. One was about a will-o'-the-wisp that floated over that swamp. At least I always thought it was a ghost story.

Years later I found out that the will-o'-the-wisp was a flame-like light caused by gases from decaying plants in marshy areas.

One time when we visited Aunt Mary and Uncle Henry, we saw a sod house that their children had built. This gave us an idea. We dug ourselves a cave in the side of a hill. This was fun until Daddy found out and put a stop to it. He said it was too dangerous; the dirt roof might collapse, and we'd be buried.

I'd like to share my experience of milking a cow. I was a teenager and thought I could. We had a cow and some chickens where we lived. One time Daddy was late coming home from work

1

and the cow needed milking. Well, David (my brother) and I decided to milk her. We also decided not to take her to the barn, but to leave her in the pasture. So, we took the pail and milking stool down to the pasture. David was holding the cow, and I was milking her when a horse fly landed on her back. David swatted the horse fly and said, "Get out of here!" The cow gingerly stepped over the bucket and walked away. That was the end of my milking a cow. When Daddy came home, he saw how much milk we had and decided she didn't need milked again that night.

Joe Davis and Family
A Farm Story

        At the beginning of summer vacation every year growing up I
would hear how my friends were planning vacations to exotic places
like Myrtle Beach and Hawaii. I could only respond with, "We're
going back to Pennsylvania" this summer, just like last summer and
the summer before that. My brother felt the same disappointment as
me in not seeing these exotic places. Each summer my parents would
drag me and my brother (we didn't want to) 3 hours away from our
friends and lives in Ohio, to the middle of nowhere Pennsylvania to
visit strange people that we didn't know. My parents called these
strange people family. We would load up our leased minivan with
Jolly Ranchers, starbursts and other candies along with 20 pounds of
Calvin and Hobbs comic books and hit the road for Kersey, PA. Our
parents kept leasing a different minivan every year instead of buying
one (I don't know why), but it always gave me something to talk
about. Sometimes we would drive straight through to Kersey,
sometimes we would make stops in Pymatuning State Park to feed the
ducks or stop in Brookville PA to get Straub's Beer or stop in
Foxburg to eat along the Allegheny River. With Beatles music
playing in the car my mom would talk about what's going on at the
farm (is there a shed being torn down, are we going on a 20-mile
hike), while my dad drove, and my brother and I smashed half eaten
jolly ranchers into the car's upholstery.

After the long and cramped drive, we would arrive at the farm (usually after dark) and be immediately welcomed to a large bonfire with a bunch of dark figures around it. The dark figures weren't important to me, but the fire, that was the main attraction. I have always been curious about fire. What is it? What are the chemical reactions involved? Why does it make the air glow? So, this became my laboratory. Finally, here was my chance to harness fire. Do rocks burn? Do beer bottles burn? How close to a flame can you get before you get burnt? Let's find out. So, while the adults sat around drinking and talking either family history or the weather, I would run my fire experiments. My brother would follow in lighting random stuff on fire because, why not? After a long while of burning myself and waving flaming sticks around, the under the influence adults would shepherd us to bed.

Sleep came quickly at the Farm. You would blink and it would be the next morning. In the morning my parents would dress my brother and I up in another pair of wood smoked clothes with fresh socks. I was told this was because my parents had ceremonially burned yesterday's socks in the fire as is tradition. We did not shower because "they are only going to get dirty again". Early every morning my dad would drive down to the country gas station 1-mile away to get morning coffee for my mother and him. I would sometimes go with him to get ice cream for breakfast. Once awake, dressed and fed the main purpose of trip began. This varied from trip to trip, but some highlights include helping to tear down an old tractor shed, going on a 5-mile hike to Byrnedale, having a family reunion, or getting ready for the 4th of July fireworks. Either way it meant getting really dirty and having mom burn more of my clothes. During one of these hikes my grandpa gave me and my brother a machete. We would stop every 50 feet to chop down a 2-inch-thick (or so) tree then drag the tree for a while. Now, this was a power we

4

couldn't do in suburban Ohio. None of our friends got to hike with a machete. My brother and I always had a tradition of finding our favorite (20 ft) stick during these hikes and dragging this stick with us for the rest of the hike. Our father would say "No, that stick is not going in the car" as we would try and sneak it home to Ohio. Sometimes we were successful, sometimes the stick ended up in the fire. Either way, the sound of the stick dragging on the ground for mile after mile raised questions with everyone involved.

No matter the purpose, some things just had to be done every trip. This included the traditional 2-mile hike to the pump house, following in Alfred's footsteps. I didn't know who this Alfred fellow was, but he must have been really thirsty to walk 2 miles every day for water. During the walk I would hear stories of how Alfred and Nips lived at the farm before both of them passed, and how the farm was very important to family history. Family history was everywhere at the farm. They had these big 2-inch-thick binders titled "Dietz Family History" with lots of black and white pictures in them. It was cool to hear the story of our lives and what made me, me. I would hear stories about how the farmhouse was first powered by power lines that my relatives made themselves and how the first barn had caught on fire and how there used to be a lumbermill on the property. I heard how someone with false teeth fell into the pond by the fire, fished out their teeth and placed them back in their mouth. These were much better stories than what I was learning in history class in school.

What I really liked about the farm was all of the open space. After spending the rest of the year in a fifth of an acre lot in the suburbs, it was a shock to be surrounded by all of this openness. There were trees and hills are far as you could see, and the sounds of traffic was replaced by the sounds of tractors and country music. Except on Sunday morning when the country music was replaced by polka music, because reasons. I felt freedom to do anything I wanted

5

in this vast stretch of openness. Mainly, I wanted to play in the fire, but to each their own, I guess.

After a few days (sometimes a week) of hiking, learning family history, and burning my fingers, we would all say our goodbyes and head on back home. My parents would pack our minivan with dirt covered clothes, mud covered hiking boots, and random sticks that my brother and I insisted we bring back home. The whole van smelled of woodsmoke, which my mom said was a good thing. We would head on back to our boring life in the crammed suburbs of Ohio armed with stories of fire and machetes and false teeth to tell everyone at school. These were much better stories than visiting the water parks of Myrtle Beach. Which was good news because parents said we were heading back next year.

Eva Long

I am Philip Dietz's oldest daughter. There are 13 of us (one deceased) so hopefully, you will hear from more of us.

I wrote a book through Storyworth, (my daughter's Christmas present to me one year.) This organization sends a question a week through e-mail for 52 weeks and you answer it. You have the option to change the question if you want. Pictures can be included. My book is 6"x9" and 332 pages with a hard cover. It was fun to do and is a treasure.

I also collected stories from my family (nieces and nephews included) and published a newsletter every month for 26 years.

Memories of the farm

Grandma had a rocking chair in the kitchen by the cook stove which I remember Uncle Alfred sitting in. (I have one in my kitchen dining area because of this.) No one was allowed in the parlor except on rare occasions and listen to the player piano. There was a room divider between the living room and dining room with bookcases on the bottom. I remember the "Hardy Boys" and the "Bobbsey Twins" were books that I read when I stayed with her a week one summer.

As a child I always thought the pond was huge. I loved the boat rides across it.

I have sister Lucy. She is a doll dressed as a nun, and I pushed her around in a wicker carriage. I think she was given to me when Grandma passed away. I once asked Aunt Anna Mae about her. She told me that Aunt Mary made the "habit" for an old doll what was in the house. Grandma was sick at the time and the doll was put on the dresser in her bedroom.

One summer my siblings and I gathered all the old split rails from a fence and built a playhouse tall enough for us to stand up in. We used some old tin roofing for a roof. This was fun until Uncle Ralph came to visit, and he asked Daddy what a pig pen was doing in that area. You will recall Uncle Ralph raised pigs.

The summer Rosemary had a family reunion; gypsy moths were everywhere. I am very squeamish about worms. They give me the chills. I found out our cousin Eva felt the same way.

A vivid memory is Uncle Frances drinking coffee out of a white cereal bowl.

These are a few of my memories.

William J (Bill) Ferris
Farm Memories from World War II

My mother was Gertrude Dietz, and my father was William Ferris. I was born in 1942, shortly after WW II was declared. My father entered the Navy and was stationed at Philadelphia Naval Hospital before being sent overseas to participate in the Pacific front. At the same time, my mother and I went to live out the war years on the farm until his return.

Although his location was undisclosed, he promised Gertrude he would send her his location in a cleverly disguised letter. Later, she exclaimed with delight, "He's in Hawaii!" She had pieced it together from the first letters of each sentence in his letter: 'How everyone was. Are you doing alright on the farm? What are you doing now?' Amazingly, these simple sentences from a sailor went undetected by Navy censors.

The farm was run entirely by Uncle Alfred, whose sole responsibility was the farm, although he had a part-time job maintaining the Dagus water supply he serviced daily. Visitors to the farm have fond memories of walking with Uncle Alfred to the pump. I remember many walks to the pump with Uncle Alfred in the winter snow and the summer heat along the dusty road that became fern lined as you progressed deeper into the woods, opening to a clearing as you neared the pump's location.

9

As the farm was located on the outskirts of the small village of Kersey, life there was isolated since no other families lived within miles. Three adults lived on the farm: my uncle Alfred, mother, and grandmother. I was the only child. Uncle Alfred became a father figure, and my only companion was his dog, Teddy. I was allowed to roam freely, playing in the fields and orchard, but always alone, save for the dog. Although farming is highly labor-intensive, I was too young to be charged with any arduous tasks, and though lonely, my life was carefree.

Alfred's brother, Uncle Cornelius, also lived at the farm. He served in the Army during the war, returned to the farm after the war, and had a full-time factory job in St. Mary's until his retirement. Neither Alfred nor Cornelius married, and while Alfred was like a father, Cornelius, upon his return from military service, was the opposite, considering me a nuisance, a brat, and an unwanted guest.

During the war, factories shifted automobile production to manufacturing war vehicles ranging from trucks to airplanes. New cars were unavailable, and essentials such as tires and fuel were rationed. Fortunately, farmers were exempt from fuel rationing as their crop and dairy production was deemed essential to the war effort. Our situation mirrored that of most small farmers at the time, with food being abundant but cash in short supply.

Others will recall Alfred's neighbor and fellow farmer Jim Steinbiser as they shared duties helping each other with equipment needs and harvesting assistance during the busy summer. During this or shortly after the war's end, the farm transitioned from horses to tractors as the motive power for plowing, planting, cultivating, and harvesting. The farm got its first tractor, a bright orange Allis

Chalmers, sometime after the end of the war. The new tractor came with a plow and cultivating attachments. Most farmers still used some horse-drawn equipment requiring two people to operate, one to drive the tractor and another to sit on the equipment to operate the controls. In later years, as I returned to the farm during the summer, I was tasked with either driving the tractor or operating the equipment, usually a sickle bar mower.

When the war ended, my father came for us, and we moved to Rosston (Ford City) to be close to his job and live with his parents. Allegheny Ludlum Steel employed him in Brackenridge before the war, so his job still existed. Postwar housing was in extreme demand as returning GIs started their families. Rental property was even more scarce, and no one would rent to a family with children, so we lived with our grandparents until I was in my teens. My parents later moved to Brackenridge, adjacent to the steel mill where my father worked until his retirement.

I have fond memories of returning to the farm during the summer to help with harvesting. Although there were tractors and other powered equipment, the tasks were extremely labor intensive, and even as a young person, I found the work brutal. I still enjoyed farm life and wanted a career in agriculture, much to the dismay of my father, who was extremely opposed and considered this a disastrous choice.

To combat this, he sent me to work with Uncle Francie Gahr for what he considered a real taste of farm life. After spending three summers there, I realized that as a small farm operator, no matter how hard you worked, you were at or near the poverty line without an outside source of income. Farm life lost its charm for me, and even

today, I do not garden or mow the lawn. I pursued an education,
which led to a profitable and satisfying career.

Bill Ferris
More Farm Musings

My father worked his entire life in an industrial position
without experiencing a serious accident or injury. He was always
highly safety conscious and instilled this mindset in me. Contrast this
with my experiences on the farm, where safety was taken lightly and
frequently considered a nuisance. Pesticides, fertilizers, and other
chemicals were handled without consideration for the hazards they
presented, and personal protection equipment was unheard of.
Shields and guards on machinery were removed when equipment
became jammed and rarely replaced, exposing sharp blades, whirling
chains, and clashing gears, all anxious to attack a carelessly placed
finger or piece of loose clothing.

The farm had an ancient Chevrolet stake body truck
purchased from J.J. Malone, the local beer distributor, when he
updated his equipment. As this truck was used for occasional hay
hauling, its battery would frequently go dead, requiring the vehicle to
be started by hand cranking. Since my task was to drive the truck, I
was responsible for cranking it. I had no idea how to do this, so
following the technique I had seen in old black-and-white movies, I
grabbed the crank firmly with both hands and spun it vigorously—only
to be met with panicked shouts from onlookers.
"What the hell are you doing, trying to kill yourself?" Such an
admonition from people who took safety so casually immediately

13

caught my attention, so I stopped only then to be educated appropriately by Uncle Alfred and Jim Steinbiser on the correct and safe procedure to crank start an engine. Despite the ancient truck's equally ancient six-volt battery having long since exceeded its service life, we could start the truck manually and use it the rest of the day to haul hay.

The lesson from that day extended beyond the farmyard. I came to see how risk permeates every aspect of life, often in ways we don't anticipate, and that unseen dangers—whether in farm work, relationships, or financial decisions—can lurk where we least expect them. I also understood that expectations vary wildly between individuals and that unseen dangers can lurk in any course of action. Sometimes, what seems obvious to others remains hidden to us until experience forces a lesson upon us.

Gregg Ferris
Mudholes

Can anything appear to be of less interest than mud holes?

Yet among the many memories of times past at the farm, there remains to me one in which common mud holes played a prominent role.

In the late 1960s, the exact year escapes me, I, along with my mother Gertrude and my sister Sue, were spending several weeks at the farm.

Late one morning, Alfred hitched the iron-wheeled, wooden cart to the larger of his two tractors, the Farmall. He and I drove the short distance to the first gate which lay at the top of a slight ridge. We passed through, continued at a northeasterly direction, and soon reached the tree line.

The road to the first gate was, at that time, dirt. An uneven path, this road was pitted with depressions large and small, each of which would transform into mud holes after a rain. A traversal of this track was at once both bumpy and sloshy.

Interestingly enough, these small ponds did not contain any of the schools of tadpoles which were found in great number in similarly sized pools that one found further back in the woods. Perhaps a biologist more familiar with the fauna of the region could explain why this was so. I suspect that excessive direct sunlight would make for a poor nursery, but I digress.

I mention the absence of tadpoles only to assure the sensitive among us today that no life was taken during this expedition.

At the tree line, Alfred and I descended from the tractor. Following both his instructions and example, I began to gather platter sized flat rocks and to place them in the cart.

I had no idea why we were doing this, but totally confident in my uncle, I remained silent and proceeded at a healthy clip, gathering and loading.

Alfred must have anticipated my unasked question, as he soon informed me that we were going to fill in some of these perennial mud pits.

Now, to a boy of 11 or 12, filling in mud holes was just as agreeable as walking through them, so I continued at my youthful pace.

In hindsight, the rocks that we gathered were not the best choice, as, consisting mainly of shale, they were themselves, in effect, long dried, compressed mud. They would serve only for a matter of months to repair the road divots. But to be fair, they were what was freely and readily available.

The load nearly complete, I was disconcerted to look up and see that we were surrounded by cows.

A dozen or so of Alfred's bovines had trooped over from the pond in the back pasture, from the area that older relatives referred to as the shingle mill.

At this pond, the cows had been enjoying their own version of a mud hole.

Surrounding us, they simply regarded Alfred and myself. Whether they had come due to boredom, from curiosity, are cows curious, or expecting food, I am not sure, even today. Had they been attracted by the dull sounds of rocks colliding with wood? Who knows.

Me, I like to think that the cows saw themselves as co-managers of the farm. While they normally confined their duties to trimming and fertilizing the pastures, in this instance they seemed to project a keen interest in the general state of the family estate, road conditions included. It's obvious that Alfred raised and retained superior cattle.

The loading was soon complete, and we retraced our steps, stopping periodically to place carefully the rocks in the soon to be former mud holes.

Of course, being only 11 or so, I did toss a few of them from afar, the flat rocks making cannonball splashes as they landed in the water.

Neither Alfred nor the cattle objected.

Sometimes I wish, as we all do, that moments like that lasted forever.

Sandy Blomgren

As long as I can remember, we always referred to my
mother's (Anna Mae Dietz Parmigiani) homestead as "The Farm".

During my growing up years, we would visit my Uncle Alfred
and Uncle Nips (Cornelius) at The Farm every Sunday afternoon. I
remember sitting on the stool beside the big old coal stove in the
kitchen and stealing ginger snap cookies which my Uncle Nips always
kept in the bottom cupboard. I also remember playing cards
(Canasta) with my Uncle Alfred, Cousin Annie Murnaghan, my mom
and my sister Jane. I would also walk down the path to the barn to see
the cows and look for barn cats. (*Upper photo on rear cover*)

I also remember that every summer my Aunt Gertrude,
Cousin Sue and Cousin Gregg Ferris would come for a visit to The
Farm and stay a couple weeks. My mother, sister, brother and I
would go out to The Farm every day while they were there. Those
were fun times. Cookouts around the campfire, going in the pond in
the wooden boat that Uncle Alfred had made, riding Pierre Pontzer's
horses with Cousin Gregg, and going for rides on dirt roads in my
dad's old van. Sometimes during my Aunt Gertrude's visits at The
Farm, my Uncle Philip, Aunt Alice and some of their children would
come visit for the day. We always referred to their children as "The
Dietz Kids" and we had a lot of fun when they visited.

One of my best memories of The Farm was when my Uncle Alfred's horse Dolly gave birth to a colt. We named the new foal Rowdy. (*Lower photo on rear cover*)

Gini Thomas
Memories of Home

Where do you begin? At the beginning I suppose. My first memories of the old homestead. I remember being very young (1 wasn't in school yet) and driving up this very long lane. At the end was "THE HOUSE". I think we all fell in love with it from the start. The yard -- well there was no yard--was weeds, very tall weeds held up by all kinds of junk, some of which were old brass bedsteads.

I remember thinking, "What a fun place to explore."

Downstairs there were two rooms: the kitchen and the living room and everything was so plain. Of course it didn't stay that way long. You know Mother. And her paint brush. We would come home and never know what color each room would be. Upstairs was a great "Pink" room that had the only closet. The closet had two doors with locks, and we took turns hiding in it and having the others lock us in. The house had a great echo as we raced through. Up and down the stairs, in and out of rooms...what fun. And the attic was a great place to scare Eva.

She was always afraid of everything, especially the dark. We loved to go upstairs and turn out all the lights and make Eva go up by herself. We would turn off the stair light at the top, then run down and when Eva wanted to go up the light wouldn't work from the bottom. Well, she got even with us. She would tell Daddy, and we would have to go up and turn on all the lights for her. To us kids this old house seemed to be the perfect place. Well, I guess it seemed that way to Mother and Daddy, too. It was OURS!!!

The house had the best banister for sliding down. Of course, the trick was to not get caught. But you know that mothers have eyes in the back of their heads and know everything. We usually got caught, probably because we never did anything quietly. We got our revenge many years later. The summer before Mother sold the house, Don and I captured Mother on video tape sliding down that very same banister. The house also had the neatest shelf in the stairway for us to swing on.

Of course we got in trouble for that too. We were going to bring the house down by hanging on the shelf. As we got older, and our legs got longer the shelf lost its magic.

In the very early years, Mother and Daddy would take us to the sand mountain to play. We thought that we had the best sand box in the world. We would always take a tub of new sand home with us.

Over the years the yard became bigger and bigger. Mother not only handled a MEAN paint brush, but also a MEAN lawn mower. At first, she only had an old push mower...and I mean really PUSH. No power then.

I remember the fun of taking off layer and layer of wallpaper in the "Pink" room. In places we found 15 or 20 layers. We tried to get as large of pieces off as we could.

We made up stories of who lived there when each layer was put on. Most of our childhood was stories and make-believe and we were happy. We didn't even know that we were "poor".

All of us had our favorite bedrooms, but we never stayed in them long. I don't remember why, but I remember moving from bedroom to bedroom from time to time.

We all had a chance to claim each of the rooms (except Mother's and Daddy's) as our own domain. The front bedroom that I always remember as being "Gold" was always Mother's and Daddy's room. Of course, the NEW babies always slept there for a time.

My favorite room was "Dolly's" room. I liked it because it had a cupboard, and it had front and back windows and doors. I guess I felt a need to escape at times. We couldn't use this room in the winter because it was too cold as it was exposed on three sides and not over a heated section of the house. This was the room (and the one next to it) that we always said, "If the house burned down, we could go up and live with Dolly." We usually said this when we were bad and got caught playing in one of the fireplaces. Dolly Walker was part of the family that we bought the house from, and she stayed with us for a while in those two rooms, so they became "Dolly's".

The front room over the kitchen was the "Pink" room and it also was a favorite of mine. I was in it more than the other rooms when I was little. There was a picture of a ship in the moonlight that used to hang in that room. I always felt that as long as I could wake and see that ship in the moonlight, I was safe. Especially on cold winter moonlight nights. That room is also the room where we had visits from the lady in the window. When I was little, I never told anyone about it because I thought it was just my overworked imagination. But later others saw her too. She was a friendly lady and never scared me. I am sure that the old house is full of "ghosts".

We used to pretend that there were "Boosts" in the attic. I think the term came from a combination of the word ghost and spook. We would run up the attic stairs and then scare ourselves and come running down yelling that the "Boosts" were after us.

The winters were fun. The day usually started with the sound of Daddy shaking out the ashes and starting the fire to warm the kitchen for us. We would then jump out from under our mountain of covers and quickly put on warm clothes and run down to the stove. Some mornings it was just too cold, and we didn't want to get up. On Sunday afternoons in the winter Daddy and Mother would make pies, doughnuts, cookies and French fries. Sometimes Daddy would make his special fudge or taffy.

We loved it when he made taffy because we got to help. Of course, the candy was never the same color when we were done with it. We pulled and pulled and played and played with it. Daddy was smart and kept some for him to pull so that we would have some to eat later. Another fun thing was to clean the stove lids, build up the fire and make potato chips. We would slice potatoes as thin as we could then put them on the red-hot lids and flip them quickly. They were sure good. Of course, we also had a few burned fingers in the process.

In the winter we doubled-up (sometimes tripled-up) in our beds to stay warm. When we were very little, I remember David, Eva and I sharing a room and we never went to bed quietly. We always had to "act up" a little. Well, Daddy would open the stair door and say, "All right, pipe down," then close the door and we would be quiet for a short time. Then someone would hit or pinch the other and there we would go again. The stair door would open, and we would hear, "OK pipe down." and the door would close. This would only happen three times. I guess that's where the expression "Three strikes and you're out" came from.

Well, one night we heard the door open the third time and we knew we were in trouble. We all ducked under the covers and up the stairs came Daddy and the razor strap. David and I got spanked and Eva stayed under the covers. Through our tears, we asked, "What about Eva?" The response was as always, "She's asleep, can't you see?" Eva usually knew she could get away with just about anything with Daddy. That's probably where we came up with the saying "Eva always was an only child." She definitely was Daddy's favorite as a child, although he loved us all equally.

David and I usually got even, somehow. We would wait till Mother and Daddy were not home to do something. We figured if we were going to get blamed for "everything", we might as well do "something". We probably deserved some of the blame. Like the times we operated on Eva's dolls. They were never the same, but we felt we saved their lives. After all they were sick. Sometimes it was their eyes, their tonsils or their appendix. In all cases they "lived"." even though their mother (Eva) wasn't very happy with our care of her babies. It they had IT - IT was meant to be operated on.

Winter also meant Christmas. We usually had very little at Christmas time, but we never knew it. We could always have several trees. We would take an ax and sled and go hunting trees. Christmas time meant decorating the tree and house and the aroma of wonderful food. We also had candy. Christmas was one of the few times we had candy and really were allowed to eat as much as we wanted on Christmas Day. Of course, we always had tummy aches, too. I remember at Christmas finding a tangerine in the toe of our stocking. Tangerines were almost gold to us as it was the only time that we had them.

In the winter, we usually had oatmeal for breakfast, and I hated oatmeal. I came up with the perfect way to not eat it. I would convince the little kids that if they didn't eat the oatmeal, I could make cookies after school with the leftover. So, if they didn't eat their oatmeal I didn't have to. Besides the cookies were much better. You can always bribe kids with cookies. I learned that very early.

Other seasons had wonderful memories too. I remember telling what month it was by which berries were ready for picking. We always had a zillion berries. We would go picking and Mother would make jam with the ones that made it home. One time we had a calf that Daddy brought home to us because she was blind in one eye and Mr. Woolverton had to get rid of her. She followed us around like a dog and loved to go strawberry picking. Just as we would reach for a berry there would be her tongue gobbling up the very berry we were reaching for. We named her Betsy after Davy Crockett's gun. Why, I don't know.

Daddy worked for Mr. Wolverton for a while and Mr. Wolverton had an employee named Andy. Andy had this great big old car and used to take us for rides and buy us ice cream.

In June, it would be strawberries; every open space seemed to be filled with berries.

In July, there were raspberries. These were my favorites, and also hard to get to, but that didn't make any difference. In August, we had blackberries and elderberries.

Daddy liked both of these. He had an old crock in the cellar that he made his own homemade wine in. Berry season also meant that Mother would make Marion Bidwell's berry cobbler for us. She also made it with peaches.

Summertime meant that the big old shutters would be shut against the hot sun. I remember the coolness of the house with the windows all open and the shutters closed as we played in our rooms. Summertime also meant thunderstorms, which I loved. We would sit on the porch and watch the lightning. We had a dog named Butzie that was afraid of the storms. He would tear out the cellar window to get in out of the storms. He also hated to get his feet wet and would wait on the porch for us when it rained. On clear days he would run up the lane to meet us after school.

Summer storms also were scary at times too. I remember a couple of times that lightning came in on the pump in a big ball and cracked real loud in the kitchen. Fun times in the storms were at night when we had to light lanterns because the lights were out. This was also good times for scary stories.

Summertime was also for going to Grandma's. It would always be an all-day trip. We would pack a picnic lunch and all pile in the car and off to Grandma's. Well, we never told Grandma that we were coming, but there she would be sitting on the porch waiting for us. She would always say, "I thought you would be here today." Of course, Grandpa would also give us all whisker rubs. Grandma always had bread and butter pickles and homemade jam for us.

In the fall, I remember the old barn full of hay. It smelled so good. It was a fun and dangerous place to play. We would walk on the beams and jump into the hay. Of course, we got carried away with dares. There was also a granary where we kept the bunnies. It seemed that we always had plenty of pets and always bunnies.

David and I usually liked to play outside and/or in Daddy's shop. But Eva would only let us get away with that for a short time and THEN we had to play with her. That usually meant playing school and/or sewing. Regardless of what we played with her, SHE was always the boss. We usually got away as soon as we could.

One time David and I did a scientific study of Stanley Glue. Everything that could be glued was. Stanley glue really stood the tests and eventually it disappeared from our sight. I wonder why? Maybe something got glued that shouldn't have.

We also built a really cool log cabin. It even had two stories and was near where Ruth's house is. We were really proud of it until one of our uncle's called it a pigpen. I can't remember which one, but David probably does. That hurt and we quit playing in it. Oh well, we moved on to better things.

We hunted for "Beavers" down in the pasture along the creek. Our beavers were big broad leaves (only certain kinds could be beavers). That pasture holds a lot of fun memories. It was a magical place. We played in the big willow. It became houses, castles, forts and whatever we needed at the time. We usually got in trouble for playing in the pasture because it involved WATER and what kid can avoid WATER. If it's there it's meant to be played in.

In the winter when the well at the house would go dry, we would load the big canner on the sled and go to the spring in the pasture. Fortunately, this did not happen too often. At first it was fun, but then it became work. Especially when it was so cold and icy.

In the fall, the pasture was loaded with beautiful flowers such as golden rods, asters, and some we didn't know. If we didn't know we would always drag them home and Mother would tell us what they were. SHE knew everything.

As we grew, we knew how lucky we were to have eighty acres to call our own. It held endless wonders. We always named everything. Such as "Birdtown", which was up above where the new barn was built. One time after we visited Uncle Henry and Aunt Mary and saw that their kids had built a sod (cave) house, we came home and built one of our own up in Birdtown. I was never comfortable going inside it. But we were proud of it.

We had "Dogwood Hollow" where Ruth's house is and we played there a lot especially when the dogwood were in bloom. We laid out sticks and logs and formed a house.

We once found a deer there and thought we should keep it. Daddy said that it was probably sick, and we should stay away from it. We wanted to nurse it and keep it, but Daddy knew best, and he killed and buried it.

We made leaf houses under the big maple at the top of the hill every fall. We couldn't wait for the leaves to fall. This tree also provided us with maple sap each winter for our maple syrup. Daddy would get out the wooden spouts that he made as soon as we had a frost, and we took turns emptying the wooden buckets into the big iron kettle. We built a fire in the front yard and boiled down the sap. Then we took it into the house and put it on the back of the coal stove and continued boiling. What a great treat when it was done. If we poured it on the clean snow, it made wonderful candy.

Winters were magic times. When the snow came, we were ready with our gloves, boots, coats and sleds. In the winter there were always wet boots, gloves and scarves drying behind the living room stove waiting for some little kid (or big kid) to go back out into the wonderful cold world and play and play. We used to go up the old road behind the old barn (where the sawmill was) and sled ride all the way the end of the lane when the conditions were right. Also, as we got older, we were allowed to go out at night when the moon was out. It was clear and crisp and perfect for a walk in the woods. It was scary but fun. It would be so cold that each step could be heard scrunching on the crust on the snow. These were good walks for telling scary stories.

Sometimes we even scared ourselves and had to run all the way home. The moon does something for scary stories, it seems to make them even better. Sometimes we would hear an animal sound and that would do it! Time to head for home.

Springtime was great, too. We would always go for walks and look for the very first wildflowers. Wildflowers are very hard to find. They always are very delicate and hide themselves well. When we found special ones, we would always take a sample home to press and put in our flower scrap book. The best hunting place was the pine woods and all the way down to the creek. Of course, we sometimes got distracted by the grapevine swing over the creek. Usually, one of us just happened to fall into the water as we swung over. Of course, it was an accident. You see what I mean about water. It seems to attract kids. All the way home we would try to make up the best story about the accident. Of course, Mother was always waiting for some story.

One time on the way back I remember planting a tiny hemlock seething in a big old tree stump. Every time we went over to the pine woods, I would make sure it was still growing.

In May of every year, Mother would make a May Altar for us. It was our job to keep flowers on it. She had a little table with a white cloth and a statue of Mary and votive candles on it. My favorite flower was the violet and there were a million of them each year on the hill directly behind the house. The hillside would be blue. We could pick for hours and never destroy the beauty. There was wide range of shades of blues and purples, and we tried to get as many different shades as we could. You could sit in one spot and pick for a long time. We also tried to find the one with the longest stem. Sometimes the stems would be almost a foot long when the grass and weeds were high. Those beautiful brave little flowers just loved to stick their heads above everything else. Mother had a white dish about four or five inches across. This is the dish I kept full of violets for the altar.

There used to be an old spring house in front of the house by the first driveway. We would make homemade root beer, bottle it and put it in the spring house to cool. There was a trough that the water from the spring used to run into, and it was shallow enough to lay the bottles in. The only drawback was that a big old black snake lived in the spring house. The root beer usually didn't last too long. We could never wait for it to ferment.

I remember the house changing as we grew older. Mother loved to knock out walls and change things. We never knew when we came home where the rooms would be. One time she went too far and knocked out a load bearing beam while making the living room bigger. Don and I captured Mother's very own rendition of this story on video tape. Daddy was cool though. Daddy was always cool. He just put up a stone pillar in the right spot and Mother had her bigger living room. Daddy in the process lost his workshop. We loved that part of the living room because of the big stone fireplace. It was fun to build a big roaring fire and sit in the heat. We also burned out the chimney several times with our exuberance.

As I got older the memories related directly to that wonderful old house are fewer. Probably because as we get older, we spend more time away from home. As a junior in high school, I worked at Camp Barree one summer and met a friend named Kirsten. She was fascinated with my family and desperately wanted to meet them all. Well, one day when we were off duty we decided to walk home from camp. We started off through the woods in what 1 knew was in the right direction. We didn't follow the road because we figured that would take too long. To this day, I don't know how we made it home, but we did. Boy, were Mother and Daddy surprised and shocked to see us come up the lane. We were in trouble, but Kirsten charmed everyone and all was better. They took us back to camp and said that if we wanted to come home THEY would come and get us. Kirsten spent a lot of time with us. She loved the big family. She only had a sister.

Another time I brought a friend named Linda home. Well, the kids told her they wanted to play cowboys and Indians, and she could be a cowboy. She loved the kids too and would go along with just about anything. That day they took her up into the woods and tied her to a stake and were building a fire around her when we rescued her. I do believe she didn't think the little monsters were serious. We got our ponies Ginger and Petty from Linda's dad. He wanted one of my paintings (yes, I, too, painted at one time) and I kept putting him off. He said he would buy it, and I said it wasn't for sale. He had built a new home and wanted it for his wife for the living room. It still wasn't for sale. Well, one day he mentioned Ponies and my ears perked up. I said, "How many ponies?" He said, "Two and you can pick them out yourself."

OK, now we had a deal. Daddy was so excited, and he went up to Morristown to Mr. Carr's, and picked out the two he wanted. He picked a brown and white one the kids named Ginger and a little black one with white pantaloons that they called Petty.

I remember how excited Daddy was when he bought them home and unloaded the truck. Of course, all the kids were too, especially Ruth. She and Daddy loved horses as much as I always did. When I was little, I pretended that I had a horse. Linda and I

29

remained friends for many years, and she still loved to come and play, but she was careful not to let herself be tied to a tree.

Well, I thought this was going to be tough assignment. But surprise, the more I write the more I remember. There're actually too many good memories to put on paper. We were very lucky kids.

Gregg Ferris
Scents and Sounds

In memory, sounds and scents are locked away
The last to depart, or so they say.
In the mind's cookbook, recipes are seared
While ingredients themselves have disappeared.

So it is with this rhythmic reflection,
Sounds and scents that I recall with affection.
Poultry at dawn wakes me at morning
When chickens arise and red rooster crows warning.

Their now absent coop was a wooden abode
Clean and dry, always dry, where only two leggers trod.
Hens would deliver that day's news in clucking bursts
Difficult to decipher, but they had it first.

In the near neighboring barn rested the cattle
Safe in the straw when the winter winds did rattle.
In the bullpen, like ballplayers masticating
They'd chew and breathe softly, patiently waiting.

In summer pasture, these bovines did browse and drink
Their melodious bells I still hear, methinks.
Return to the barn, where cut green grass turns gold
Its scent more sweet as it dries and grows old.

Next to the mow, oats lay like kittens at nap
Tranquil 'til shoveled into sacks of burlap.
Then they would murmur and fuss
Rolling from the blade while kicking up dust.

Each farm building had its own perfumes
Some with unique odors in every room.
The house itself with tobacco varnish
It was there for years, sadly to vanish.

The aroma of Alfred's rolled cigarettes
Tobacco has proved deadly, and yet...
I'd like to find and ignite his brand
And bring his presence closer to hand.

The cellar's preserve of potatoes and meat
Would welcome the visitor with the smallest of feet.
It sometimes smelled of cardboard and beer
Strangely compelling, but nothing to fear.

Other places come rushing to mind
Earthy tractor and tool sheds, you no longer find.
In the shed, the small tractor would cough, 'No, thanks'
As Alfred would smoke, and continue to crank.

The woodshed and shop somewhat like twins
The fragrance of chips, whichever you're in.
 Far away, past fields, dark woods, and pungent ferns,
The pump, musty dusty concrete, where water did churn.

Then back to the white house, dinner not afar
The wind, rustling treetops, resembles a car.
Later that evening, flames of fire
Crackle and wave with unfettered desire.

In order to whisper, somewhat eerily,
But importantly, this is family.

Gregg Ferris
A Glass of Milk

It's a childhood memory, triggered by a glance at a piece of furniture in my home.

I was seated, along with my two older siblings on the bench, a plain, homemade set of wooden planks, painted in white, not oyster or ivory, but white. The seating surface was covered in what we called contact paper, but which was more or less an adhesive backed shelving paper. It had the advantage of facilitating sliding as we sat and exited en masse with little danger of acquiring a sliver in the rump.

Placed between the massive, thick-legged kitchen table and the wall, beyond which lay the cellar stairs.

The bench accommodated three or four children and was our preferred place for meals as we had nothing like it at home.

I myself had such fond memories of it this bench seat that years later, I convinced my wife of the indispensability of such a piece. One was duly acquired, sadly it had to be more elegant, for our kitchenette. It is the thought that counts.

My mother poured us each a glass of fresh milk from a small cream colored, floral patterned small mouthed pitcher.

As the glasses were filled one by one, I reflected on the sequence of steps that had brought this lactic beverage to the evening's meal.

"Can you bring in one of the cows for milking?" I had been asked a few hours earlier.

My mind had replied, "Who, me?" but my lips and tongue vocalized the response as "Sure."

It was a great honor, which is shorthand for a chore that entails responsibility, one that generated a shiver despite the heat of the midday July sun.

There was no need to ask which cow, as the beast had been identified to me early in the morning when we kids had accompanied my uncle Alfred on his morning activities.

We were as much as an entourage as a nuisance for him, although to this day I am not certain where on the balance between pro and con he placed our annual two-week presence. Somewhere between a vacation and a fortnight of fever is the nearest scale that I can propose.

Back to our chosen milk giver. She, of course, we had learned that obvious distinction years previously, was black and white, and she ported real horns, an accessory that seemed to be fading rapidly from bovine fashion. Around her neck was a large, worn, brown strap, from which dangled a tarnished brass bell. Evidently, neither originated from the shelves of Tiffany's, but they served the dual purpose of positively identifying her as well as finding her easily, given the large size of the farm, whose cattle domain was comprised of open pasture in addition to many acres of woods, ideal shade during the summer months.

An hour later, I found myself alone on my mission. Quests are solitary ventures, but to be honest I was more concerned with survival than glory. I missed the comfort of my siblings, yet I concluded that if one of them had been selected instead of me, then I too would have remained absent. Although we teased each other about having been adopted, our shared sense of self-preservation demonstrated our common gene pool.

As I regarded the cow, for she had no name, a few insects, also nameless, buzzed past my head, intent on important events in their brief lives. Would mine run longer? I smelled numerous anonymous flower fragrances that combined to offer without charge the aroma of High Summer.

Would this be the sole bouquet of my impending doom? My imagination was racing at full speed, aware of its own possible demise and endeavoring to complete its own outlandish bucket list.

If this simple chore went wrong, I would be gored, and stomped, becoming part of the countryside in a way heretofore inconceivable.

I shivered again, and for a reason unknown this motion reminiscent of winter brought to my mind the song The Twelve Days of Christmas and its maid a milking.

I was a boy of nine and if an eight-year-old maid girl could milk a cow, then a boy of nine could fetch said cow. Only the following Noël did I learn the correct lyrics when I performed for the first time in a school play.

Although I remained frightened of the beast, and I assumed that it's up to now docility was a clever subterfuge, I was more afraid of failing my uncle than becoming part of his pasture.

Besides, I said to myself, I'm not defenseless.

I regarded the stick that I held in my bony hand, a tool that I had selected myself from the numerous that stood ready in the shop adjacent to the house. I had chosen the one that had struck my untrained eye as being the most capable, experienced, and proven.

My yet unstressed imagination had said derisively, "it's a bunch of sticks, pick one and let's go." Sometimes even those tasked with imagination have no creativity.

This was not just a stick, but a cattle stick. There is power in words, more so in precise words.

In the pasture, I looked at the cow and then again at my cattle stick.

It was about four feet long, as thick as my uncle's thumb, and it had the dark hue of a seasoned and polished branch of walnut.

"It is not walnut, it's birch," my mind corrected me, then it continued "the color comes from dried blood, probably from one of you cousins that they never talk about anymore."

I wanted so to switch off this annoying part of me. That was impossible, ignoring him as much as possible was the best that I could manage.

I say cow but she had friends, dozens in fact. I had located her readily enough at her favorite watering hole, which in this instance was an actual watering hole, a farm pond.

It sat at the base of three intersecting slopes and was replenished by a small stream.

It may be that courage and wisdom are found at opposite ends of life's see-saw, yet I doubt that many of us would be thrilled by or contented with a permanent seat in its pivot zone.

After coaxing, cajoling, and bizarre gestures on my part, targeted first at myself as a form of rehearsal, then directed at the cow, accompanied by bugling on her part, I was able to convince her to move.

Ten years later I would practice similar movements before dates.

Today I have no doubt that the cow was toying with me, enjoying her chance to perform before her troop with me, the debutant cowherd.

Tiring of a scene singularly lacking in memorable dialogue, being nine I had neither sophisticated language nor curses at my disposal, the cow began to move. Once she started all that remained for me to do was to congratulate myself while silently rendering thanks, and then to follow her.

It was a ten- or fifteen-minute hike back to the barn, following the well-worn cow path across the pasture, through a wooded section where the hooves of countless passing had exposed the roots of several large hemlock trees.

The path was so deep and smooth that its route through the grass on either side of it could have been followed readily in the dark.

Behind me I heard more cow bells as the entire herd was following. There were brown cows, and brown and white cows, and others with the same color pattern as mine, who I had now named Angie, at least for this trip. Angie was a sort of reddish bovine; it looked good on her. A bull followed along, but for my peace of mind I pretended that he had chosen to remain behind. Half grown calves were more difficult to ignore as they skittered in and out of procession and generally behaved as I supposed I did in similar human proceedings.

We finally entered the barn through its huge open door. I managed to guide only Angie to an open stanchion and closed it around her neck. She gave a toss of her head, causing the bell to clang as a sort of starting signal before she lowered her head to begin eating the treat of oats and buckwheat that lay before her.

Inside, the barn offered its own pleasant scent, one of fresh hay and clean straw and sleeping oats all mingled with that of free-range cattle, the sort of place a family of three could call home for a week in December.

Alfred was there, with a small, short, three-legged wooden milking stool. The sound of jetting milk squirting into a galvanized pail was evidence that the milking had commenced.

During the process, I watched Angie from a foot away. Her large eyes and broad forehead were attractive, any sign of malevolence that I had only imagined was gone.

The milking was soon complete, the galvanized bucket that I mistakenly equated with terms such as pasteurized and homogenized now full.

Alfred carried the milk to the house where he quickly strained it in a cursory manner, using relatively clean cheesecloth, into a floral pitcher saving the cream for the butter making that we kids would attempt the following day. He then set the porcelain vessel in the refrigerator.

While my uncle performed this task, I released Angie from the stanchion, and she made her way back to her companions.

My mother finished pouring the milk, and while the large, thick specks of pale-yellow cream were not to my liking, and in fact repulsed my stay behind siblings, I made sure to drink every drop of Angie's gift and to confidently request another when I had finished the first glass of milk.

The event described above was at one time in my future. Until it happened. The very best of the past used to not exist. You have to go through the future to get the past. It's the trip of a lifetime.

Eva DeGlopper

Anna Krellner (or Grellner) was born in Hollenberg, in Bavaria. She arrived at Ellis Island in 1894 aboard the ship Westernland. According to the passenger manifest she was then 11 years old. She had at least one brother, Johann or John, who was by then a US citizen, an older sister called Margaret, and two older sisters, twins, who were each called Barbara.

As my mother told it, the twins' mother did not know that she would have two babies instead of one. She had prepared only one name for a girl. Since the smaller of the babies was frail and not expected to live, there was reason to hurry the baptism.

The priest who was to perform the baptism suggested that if one twin was to be baptized Barbara Anna, the other could be baptized under the name Anna Barbara. That was done, but the babies were called Little Barbara and Big Barbara, or to my mother, Big Aunt Barb and Little Aunt Barb. I think that it was the fragile Little Aunt Barb that my mother visited when our family went to Kersey, but Mom did not invite us to join her.

Peter and Anna were kind and generous people. If a hungry man came by Anna would prepare a meal for him to eat on the porch. If Peter had work that the man could do, like wood-chopping, he would pay the man for the work and let him sleep in the barn.

After Anna's death, one of my mother's cousins told me that Anna always welcomed visitors. The coffeepot was always full, and Anna was ready for a chat.

Uncle Alfred kept up the practice of generosity toward neighbors. We visited once in what must have been the summer of

40

1960. I had just finished my first year in college and, as we did then, taken up the grown-up habit of smoking. Smoking was sociable, so one afternoon I sat with Uncle Alfred at the kitchen table, chatting and smoking.

A neighbor boy came by, he was no more than twelve or so, looking for a pail of the milk that Alfred was giving his fatherless family. Besides the milk, the boy asked Alfred for a cigarette. Alfred gave him the paper and tobacco that he used himself and the boy expertly rolled his own.

Then Alfred offered me the makings of a roll-your-own cigarette. I thanked him but quickly went back to my own ladylike filter-tips.

Eva DeGlopper
Peter Dietz

Peter was the son of Joseph Dietz, a shoemaker. He was not well-educated; the story is that he left school at an early age by way of a window and never returned. His wife, Anna Krellner Dietz, kept the books of the farm until the children were old enough to take over that responsibility. Peter did not inherit the farm, but bought it, after working on the railroad for some time. He did well enough so that eventually he had the biggest barn in Elk County.

Peter and Anna had ten children, five girls and five boys. My mother Eva Barbara was the third child and the first girl.

In the chilly winters, Peter would get up first. Before he went out to look after the animals, he would light the coal stove for his wife so that when she got up to cook breakfast it would be to a warm kitchen. My mother said that she remembered standing on a chair when she was eight years old frying potatoes for her father.

He also bought for his wife a washing machine, not an electric machine, but one that had a crank that was turned by hand. There may also have been a churn that worked on the same principle. Peter seems to have been an early adopter of technological advances. He owned the second automobile in Kersey; the first belonged to the doctor. Neighbors called him the Flying Dutchman. Electricity went first to the barn, but soon after was installed in the house, as was a telephone. Water came from a spring-fed reservoir on the property, a reservoir that also supplied water to the nearby coal mines.

From my mother, Eva Dietz Burdick:

Peter Dietz was known to be a particularly talented horse trader. One Sunday, after word got around about a trade that worked out even more to his advantage than usual, the priest who was saying Mass gave a sermon about truthfulness. Peter, offended, got up from his seat in the pews and solemnly walked out.

Eva DeGlopper

Peter Dietz and Anna Krellner were married on September 20, 1904.

Anna had for some time been working as a caregiver for a family with a large number of children. She herself, according to her daughter Eva, had only three years of education in Germany, but she was able to teach herself English from the schoolbooks that belonged to her employer's children. I remember that in old age she spoke English with a slight, charming accent.

The first two children of the marriage were boys, my uncles Ralph and Alfred. The third was a daughter, my mother Eva Barbara, born in 1908.

According to my mother, Anna had intended to name the coming child after the saint whose feast fell on the day of the birth, but my mother was born on the feast of St. Bartholomew. The feminine version of Bartholomew that came to Anna's mind was Bertha. "Oh, no!", said Anna, "Not Big Bertha!" so she named her daughter Eva after an aunt.

Winters in Kersey could be snowy, so much so that Peter sometimes tied a rope between the house and the barn so that he could find his way back even if the snow was falling heavily.

Ordinarily the children walked to school, but if snow made the trip particularly difficult Peter would hitch horses to his sleigh and give them a ride. Eva was small for her age, so her parents kept her out of school until she was eight. My mother said that "when the kids started school," the family began to speak English at home. In her own old age, my mother remembered only one phrase: "'Raus mit dich", something her parents said when sending a child firmly to bed.

In Bavaria the women looked after the farm animals, while the men worked in the fields. Anna kept chickens and had a large garden but left the work of the barn to the men. She might nurture an orphan calf behind the coal stove, or the space might be open to a child who wanted to find a warm place to dress for school. My mother remembered breaking the ice on the washbasin in her bedroom, quickly washing her hands and face, then hurrying down to the warm kitchen.

Anna wanted at least one of her daughters to become a nun. When the eldest, Eva Barbara, reached high school age, her parents sent her to the Benedictine Academy in Saint Mary's. Like many farmers, they didn't have a lot of cash, so her father paid her tuition in coal and potatoes. She stayed with an aunt in Saint Mary's.

During one school vacation, she went home to the farmhouse, where she hosted a taffy pull for her friends, the people she went around with, both girls and boys. Her father, watching her with the boys, decided that she would never make a nun.

She finished high school at the local public school.

Eva DeGlopper

Peter Dietz was quite sick with the deadly strain of influenza that was pandemic in 1918, so sick that the family hired a nurse to look after him. The nurse had been working for a sick neighbor, but when the neighbor learned that Peter was ill, he said, "Go look after Pete Dietz, he has all those kids."

Eva, who would have been nine or ten in 1918, was interested in what the nurse was doing, so she watched her and thought, "I could do that!"

She remembered, and when she was old enough, went to work in the Sylvania plant for a year to earn money, then somehow arranged to go to nursing school in spite of her mother's qualms. Her mother took one look at the dormitory at Buffalo General Hospital (now Meyer Memorial Hospital) and, with some trepidation, asked, "Are you sure you want to stay?"

With her was her cousin Monica Herzing, also a nursing student. When Monica and Eva graduated in 1932, during the Great Depression, even nurses had a hard time finding work, so the two cousins shared a job. They shared much of their free time, too, going around in a group with other young people, including another cousin, the then seminarian Raymond Herzing. Eva had decided that she would never marry. "I was going to be a career woman", she said. One evening however, she went to a party where she met Roger Burdick, the man who would soon become her husband.

The young couple moved to West Virginia, where neighbors consulted Eva about minor illnesses, some of them calling her "Doc Burdick", but she did not work again as a nurse until almost twenty years later.

Her daughter Barbara Burdick Langlotz followed her into the nursing profession, as did Barbara's daughter Julie Langlotz Grey, and most recently Julie's daughter Courtney Hill Cartwright. Four generations of nurses!

Barbara Burdick Langlotz

My mother, Eva, occasionally told stories of the farm. She remembered the huge meals, meat and potatoes, kept in the warming oven and served to the men before they went out into the field. She talked of the unmarried women relatives who used to come live with them for a while to help in sewing clothes for the children to wear to school. She talked of blood sausage and dandelion salad. She told of having classmates over in the winter for ice skating on the pond, after Alfred had driven the team onto the ice to check ifs strength. She also said the ice from the pond was cut and hauled and stacked in one of the sheds with straw layers and would last for a very long time. She said her mother sent her to the convent school in St Mary's to become a nun, but her father said it wouldn't work, she liked the boys too much!

She gave me the pearl necklace Alfred gave her upon her graduation. I still have it. Grandma and Grandpa Dietz spoke German to each other. but only English to their children

I remember going into the basement as a child and seeing eggs, butter and baked goods stored down in that cool space. There was a spring running along one edge of the floor. I remember one time my brother John, as a child, did something Bernie thought was unfair to Anna Mae, so Bernie grabbed a huge squash and chased Jack around the yard.

Bernie told stories that scandalized my mother, Eva. She always warned me, "Don't tell Jack's kids."

According to Bernie, Peter wasn't drafted for WWI because he was a farmer. He had two brothers who didn't want to go to war, so they bought sheep and became farmers until the war ended. He also said during prohibition, times were so tough that Alfred and "Flick" Pontzer made moonshine and Black Jack Mosier sold it.

Alfred even gave Bernie the formula later in life, a ratio of 6 10 5: 6 lbs. of rye, 10 lbs. sugar, 5 gallons water, and a cake of yeast. Let work, it will bubble as though there is a fire under it. If you bottle it then, it is rye wine, if you run it through a still, you have moonshine. It was made in a chicken coop behind the barn and stored in a cistern that was located under an old saw blade.

Bernie told of the Pontzer farm having a coal mine behind the pond. They hid some moonshine in the mine which unfortunately collapsed. Later, they strip mined the area and watched nervously to make sure the hidden moonshine did not resurface!

Marlene Stroud (née Langlotz)
Memories of the Farm

I remember being one of the "city kids" who came to the farm every summer from the big city of Buffalo, New York. There were so many neat things to do there.

Climbing and jumping in the hay barn, chasing the mean old chickens and trying to find their eggs, picking blackberries in the rain, sneaking drinks of warm milk fresh from the cow with Uncle Alfred. I remember only being allowed in the boat on the pond when the adults were around.

Why did it seem like the springhouse Uncle Alfred walked to everyday was miles and miles away? When Uncle Bunk (Bernard) came to visit with his homemade wine, the adults told their best stories. I just had to sit still and keep quiet, and I got to hear them all. Why did all the beds at the farm have a big groove in the middle that we all kept rolling into when we slept 2 or 3 to a bed? Why did all the Pennsylvania cousins talk so funny? Or was it us New York cousins?

The best part of my summers growing up were the week or so we spent at the farm every year.

Barbara Langlotz
Memories of the Farm

The farmhouse with a big welcoming porch...bats at dusk flying from house to pond...everyone's favorite rocking chair by the kitchen stove...the pond with a boat, a swing, and a place for bonfires...shucking corn for the chickens...gathering eggs...Uncle Al milking cows...freshly made whipped cream...the enticing but forbidden front parlor...sliding down the banister when grandma wasn't looking...eating grandma's apple slices drying in the attic...going to the pump station...cousins, cousins, more cousins!

Finally, sharing good times with my own children.

John Parmigiani

My story takes place in the farmhouse in the early 1970s. My family visited the farmhouse routinely on Sunday afternoons during my childhood. My mother, Anna Mae Dietz Parmigiani, remained close to her brothers Cornelius (Nips) and Alfred for all of their lives.

Our weekly visits were just one of many interactions my mother had with them. In the summer our Sunday visits included many outdoor activities. In the winter most of our time was spent inside the farmhouse. Games and puzzles were common during these visits. Card games of Canasta and jigsaw puzzles were frequent. More rare were games of hide-and-seek.

Several instances of hide-and-seek that I recall occurred when I was about 8 years old. As I recall the game was initiated by one of the adults. I was the youngest attending the Sunday visits in those days and was designated as the hider. My sisters, Jane and Sandy, were the seekers. The adults (my mother, Nips, Alfred, Annie Murnaghan, and her father Henry) together selected the hiding place. The game was repeated several consecutive weeks with me hiding in the same location and my sisters searching for me.

The game was quite fun for all. My sisters enjoyed the hunt. The adults were very pleased that their selected hiding place proved to be so secretive. I was quite content to be the center of attention. I was right in the midst of all the activity but remained hidden. As I recall, my sisters were never successful in finding me and the hiding place was never revealed to them.

It's rather poignant that all the adults are now gone. I'm the only one left who remembers the hiding place or even remembers the game being played. So, where was the hiding place my sisters failed to find spent multiple Sunday afternoons?

52

It was in the kitchen. The centerpiece of the farmhouse kitchen in those days was the old cookstove. On one side was the kitchen sink and cabinetry. On the other side was the refrigerator, the door into the bathroom, and, in the corner, a bench with boots in front of it and coats on the wall behind it. My hiding place was created by placing a pair of boots on the bench and hanging a coat on the wall behind them. I would step into the boots and stand, back to the wall, with the coat hanging over my face and body and extending over the tops of the boots. Thus, I "disappeared".

Virginia (Gini) Dietz Kelley

My memories of the farm are all very positive. We did not get to visit for any length of time over the years.

As a child we would go "Up Home" as we called it every summer. I remember it taking all day with usually a picnic at a State Park along the way.

As a child from a very large family, I would spend most of the day there taking care of the younger ones. One of those times was putting a very fussy little boy named Philip in the hammock and swinging him till he fell asleep. I do remember visiting Aunt Helen and she always had fresh baked cookies for us. Uncle Francis called me "Ginger", and many years when I got the horses for the kids, they named one Ginger.

I remember Aunt Tootsie and Uncle Paul's wedding. Grandma Dietz was there. I also remember her visiting us and she always brought homemade sauerkraut for us. When she ate, I remember that she had a vein in her neck that jerked as she ate. We were little kids and always asked her to "Do that again", and she laughed at us kids.

I do not remember much else about Grandma Dietz as we lost her way too soon.

We made many visits to the farm over the years and all were wonderful. Among them:

Sitting at the table in the kitchen that was pushed back up to the door in the basement.

Visiting the house and never being allowed in the parlor. Of course, we had manners and just looked in the door.

The only time was when Grandma Dietz was laid out in the parlor, then we were allowed to go in and say goodbye.

We always over the years loved to sit by the pond on the swing. Also had rides in a boat on that pond. Still sit there when I go back.

We played in the barn and ran in the fields. Going "Up Home" was magic.

One time I went up years later with Daddy, Philip and Rob. Uncle Alfred and Uncle Nips lived there, and Daddy stopped and got hotdogs and fixings to have lunch with them.

I never got to stay there over the years, but even all the short visits were wonderful and too many to name them all.

I appreciate that Jane still lives there, and it is still HOME when we are there.

Barbara Langlotz
"City Cousins" Visit the Farm

It must have been while we lived in West Virginia that we traveled by train to visit the farm.

We had a small compartment just for us, with beds opened by a porter. The train took us to Ridgway, where Uncle Henry Murnaghan picked us up in in car, took us to his house on a hill, parked on his slanted driveway, and put blocks behind the wheels to keep the car from rolling away.

After Aunt Mary fed us, it was time for Uncle Henry to take us to the farm. We must have had southern accents because I was met with, "Say something, Barbara Ann," and then laughter.

Uncle Henry was unusual for two reasons. He heated his house with newspapers and collected player pianos. The newspapers were ends of blank newsprint rolls from the newspaper where he worked, so they were really paper logs.

The player pianos took up much of the house. I never tired of watching the piano keys going up and down, producing music without human hands.

The story about Uncle Henry heating his house with logs of newspaper must be hard to believe; my teacher did not believe me when in elementary school, I listed paper in the list of fuels. I had to have my mother verify!

Gregg Ferris
Jim's Traveling Player Piano

Barbara's above story, with its memory of Uncle Henry Murnaghan's player pianos, prompted me to add this long postscript.

Cousin James Murnaghan was the son of Henry and Mary Murnaghan.

Although I had known him since my infancy, James was 17 years my elder, and I did not really know him. That changed in the late 1990s one evening at the farm. James mentioned that he had been in Louisville (where I live) recently, attending a large semi-annual gun show. I invited him to stay with us if he traveled to the next one.

A few months later, he called and took us (my wife Karen and I) up on my offer.

James, now Jim, and I quickly became close. He stayed with us innumerable times, and we traveled together extensively. By this time, his parents were deceased, as was Annie, his sister. We visited Europe a score of times, including Ireland, which Annie had toured a few years before her death. There we met some of his cousins (Murnaghan) in Monahan county.

Jim also had cousins in Florida. He told me that he had sold the player pianos, one to a cousin in Florida. That was around the year 2000.

Jim was like an older brother to me, and I was devastated by his death in July 2021. He had selected me as executor of his will, and I spent several weeks at his home in Warren, PA, settling affairs.

One day during my stay, the phone in Jim's house rang. It was the cousin from Florida who had bought the player piano decades before, asking to speak to Jim.

57

We spoke for several minutes after he learned of Jim's passing. He, John, had called to let Jim know that the player piano had finally arrived at his house, and he had wanted to play it for Jim.

According to John, he had paid to have the piano shipped to a piano restorer in the Carolinas over 20 years previously, when it had been trucked from the Murnaghan home in Ridgway. There in the south, it had sat untouched while the restorer attended to other matters. Years went by, and the restorer died. The piano passed into control of his family, who assumed it was the restorer's property. After legal proceedings which took more years, proper ownership was determined, and the forlorn piano was forwarded to a different piano restorer, in California. An additional year or so passed, and the piano finally arrived at John's home in Florida, around the time of Jim's death.

John having recounted the story of the twenty-year traveling piano, I sat back in Jim's living room and listened as piano music wafted from the phone handset. I wonder now if it was one of the same pieces that Barbara had heard all those years before.

Barbara Langlotz
The Spring

As an adult, I liked to visit the farm while Bernie, Bernadette and Jimmy were there. Bernie used to take us on long hikes, sometimes looking for places he had known as a child.

One day, we walked and walked. Bernadette said, "Dad, are you lost?" "No," he replied, "I know where I am."

We walked and walked some more. Again, Bernadette asked, "Dad, are you sure you' re not lost?"

"No, I know where I am."

We walked and walked longer and eventually saw a farmhouse. At this, Bernie said, "NOW, I know where I am!"

On one of those walks, he took us to a spring deep in the woods. He said one of the Pontzers camped there during the depression, using the top of an old auto for a doghouse.

I' m not sure where we were, but I don't think a Pontzer would have reason to camp on Dietz land, so it could have been anywhere.

Later, I went to a talk given by a woman who studied hobos and wrote a book about them. She even went to their yearly convention. Yes, there are still hobos! They are different from bums. because they do odd jobs to support themselves, although they probably still ride the rails. I learned that one way to recognize a hobo camp is by a water source in a secluded spot that is not too far away from railroad tracks; this fit the spot Bernie had led us to. I really wondered about the story of this spring.

Barbara Langlotz
The Forge

One time, Bernie wanted to fire up the old forge in the shed. He sent my kids out to gather coal. I'm not sure where he sent them, Dietz, or Pontzer property, which was abandoned at the time.

We had a great time, lighting the fire, pumping the bellows, hammering iron, dipping candles, and innocently melting some lead that Bernie brought, and pouring molten lead into soldier molds from my son in law Paul' s attic. As far as I know, none of us any harmful effects from the lead.

We had a great time.

Barbara Langlotz
The Wood Stove

The stove was so welcoming in the winter months we lived on the farm. The kitchen was the only room in the house that felt warm. I remember the round lids on the stove that covered the fire inside, and the lid lifter, which was used to add more wood, coal, or trash.

There was a bucket, I believe called a coal scuttle, beside the stove. This was full of coal, ready for use.

Family gatherings were held around the large kitchen table in cold months. Not just meals, but games and conversations. My favorite seat was in the rocking chair. I used to stand near it, waiting my turn.

Some of the chairs in the back of the table leaned against the cellar door, which did not close very securely, so you had to be careful or sit elsewhere.

Where did the coal for the fire come from? My mother Eva always stated that the farm had not been strip mined. Would the coal be so close to the surface that it could be collected without prior mining? Does anyone know? (*Editor's note: There was surface coal on the far side of the pond, in the 1960s*)

Bernie wanted to bake in that stove, so one time my family went to the farm with Bernie and Lenore, Bernadette and Jimmy. and did so, which was tricky. because there was no temperature control and no timer, but Bernie remembered his mother using a broom straw to gauge the oven readiness.

We baked the usual baskets of rolls. doughnuts. and such. A few were a little brown on top, but that easily scraped off. Lenore, I remember, spent her time washing all the dishes!

61

According to Bernie, the highchair was first used by Ralph. And was given a fresh coat of paint for each of the 9 subsequent children. Bernie stripped off all the paint, refinished it, recaned the chair, and used it for his own grandchild. The wheels were too small to push very far, but I suppose you could wheel it around the house with the child remaining seated.

Barbara Langlotz

When I was older, with children of my own, we often visited the farm with Bernie, Bernadette, and Jimmy.

Once, after dark, we were sitting around the kitchen table with Nips, talking, laughing and making plans. As usual, there was uncle Bunk's wine in gallon jugs and of course we were drinking.

Uncle Alfred was in bed, but suddenly he came into the kitchen, wearing his plaid felted bathrobe, and holding an alarm clock.

"Don't you people know what time it is? Why can't you make plans in the daytime?"

Bernadette and Jimmy went back to Helen's house, and the rest of us slunk upstairs; Nips losing his balance and getting an abrasion from his glasses, which were bent out of shape. A simple Band-Aid later, he made it upstairs. As far as I know, nothing more was ever said, but that was Alfred.

He told you when you were wrong, but when it was over, it was really over. He was always one of my favorite people.

Jane Parmigiani Huff
Memories of the Farm

Some of my earliest memories of the farm are when my sister Sandy, and brother John and I would come out to the farm on a weekday in the summer with our mom Anna Mae Dietz Parmigiani and meet her sister, Mary Dietz Murnaghan to clean the farmhouse.

The adults would dust and vacuum. The vacuum cleaner was a silver cannister and had a cord that had markings that reminded me of a snake. My sister and brother and I would have fun playing outside. I remember the weather being always warm and sunny.

We would play with a red wagon called Snappy Boy, the words written on its the side, and give each other rides in an old stroller down the hill that started at the top of the driveway past the front of the house. These items were kept in a small shed beside the house.

I remember hearing that vacuum when we were in the house and remember it all being such a happy time and to this day the sound of a vacuum is comforting to me. It was during summer vacation which, of course, was a happy time.

I remember catching water in Uncle Nip's silver cooking pans from the drips from the front porch during a rainstorm and going in the rowboat built by Uncle Alfred in the pond. We would watch dragon flies buzz around. We were a little afraid of them. We saw frog eggs in the pond. We would row over by the "deep part" on the back right corner of the pond.

In the spring, I heard "peepers". Years ago, I'd sit on the front porch with my orange cat Julie cat and enjoy their song. I hear them tonight.

Lighting bugs. My siblings and cousins and I would catch them in a mason jar and put aluminum foil over it with air holes and enjoy their glow. I look forward to them still. They are especially magical down beyond where Ed has the garden, the meadow towards the woods.

One time, we decided to gather a lot of the water lilies from the pond. There were too many of them. There are still too many. We had a boatload of them. But it did not really do much good. They keep spreading. But it was fun gathering them.

I remember one summer Uncle Nips got some inflatable animals to put in the pond. I think a blue whale was one of them. They looked cool in the pond.

Another very special time was when Aunt Gertrude Dietz Ferris would come with her children Gregg and Sue for two wonderful weeks in the summer.

Just sitting on the front porch is a very fond memory.

I remember the weather being warm and sunny most of the time with not a lot of rain to spoil our fun.

Snappy Boy the wagon and the stroller were also enjoyed with our cousins.

We also went hunting in "dumps" with our moms. Places on the property or neighboring property where old bottles could sometimes be found. Our mothers would have shovels and dig for treasures. We kids did not like these hunts. It was usually really hot, and we got bored with this activity however my Aunt Gertrude would always say maybe the bottles could pay for Gregg's college education. LOL.

The good old days when my mom and Aunt would get to spend some time together.

Another wonderful thing we did, and still do, is have cookouts down by the pond. We sit on the old glider and swing and benches and folding chairs and big rocks and have lots of food, including s'mores and mountain pies. We'd talk about and celebrate all sorts of things in this treasured spot.

My mom would tell scary stories to my daughter Megan and son Ernie and Cousin Jenny.

Even though we have the wrap around porch I still like to go down and sit by the fire. Sometimes the weather is too nasty for that. If weather is good, I'm going to put the food that does not need plugged in and kept hot down on the table by the cookout site and snacks and other stuff so we can continue to enjoy that tradition.

Another fond memory is going down to the barn into the corn crib and enjoying the sweet smell. Also climbing on the hay bales upstairs. And the horrible feeling on the legs when wearing shorts when your leg would go between them.

I remember seeing the cows in the barn. Each had their own special spot with the metal thing to keep them in, and the sound of them munching on the hay in the trough in front of them.

I remember looking for kittens in the barn and seeing big cats scamper upstairs in the barn. We named one cat with white and black spots Timmy. My siblings and I would coax Timmy to come close to pet from the back porch steps with small pieces of bread. Uncle Alfred would say, "He is a little shy."

Uncle Nips would have a different opinion. He would clap his hands and hiss at them, lol.

Another fun thing we did was look for berries. Strawberries would be in the field across from the top of the driveway. Our Uncle Nips had a friend named Rosemary visit during strawberry time, and we could not believe it when she said she did not like strawberries. We kids loved them.

There were also red and black raspberries. Huckleberries grew alongside the road to Gus Johnson's camp (the owner at that time), a big bush of them. This was to the right of the road leading to the barn.

I enjoyed picking apples with Mary Dietz Murnaghan and her husband Henry and their daughter Annie. The Dietz orchard was where the Elk County fairgrounds are now. Also, the Murnaghans joined us in picking huckleberries.

Another very fond memory were trips in our white van. We would pile in here at the farm. My mom Anna Mae Dietz Parmigiani and my Aunt Gertrude Ferris in the back in lawn chairs, our dog Cassidy wherever he found room, my siblings and cousin Gregg in the middle seat, my dad Paul driving and Uncle Alfred in the passenger seat and I was on the engine block cowling. No worries about annoying things like seatbelts, lol.

We had many adventures. We would go to the old stone camp. Picking blueberries, I heard a rattlesnake. Never saw it but heard it and slowly moved from the area. Also, we'd go to this big quarry waterhole and see older kids jumping in.

I remember riding with Uncle Alfred on the toolbox on the tractor when I was very young. And popping corn in a corn popper over the fire at the cookout site by the pond.

My husband Ed remembers as a child coming here with his dad and seeing the big heating grate in the living room. He also he remembers going down in the basement and seeing the potatoes in the bin and one 4th of July my Uncle Bernie Dietz making pizza in the kitchen here and that someone had the kiln going in the building we call the shop. It had at one time been a blacksmith shop.

I actually got to live here when I was an infant to one year old. This was during the time our house was being built in town in Kersey.

The finest memories and I'm so blessed to be able to live here today and continue to enjoy the farm. As the saying goes,

The path through life may often roam
Yet it's here at home that my heart feels most at
home.

Barbara Langlotz

Peter A. Dietz, I was told, escaped from school at a very young age by crawling out a window. He never returned. Supposedly, he could not read and could only sign his name.

I was very young when I met him, so I only remember he smoked a pipe. My mother, Eva, said when she had an earache, he would blow smoke into her ears to relieve the pain. Alfred also smoked, but he rolled his own cigarettes from papers and a tobacco pouch he carried in his pocket.

Farmers were exempt from the draft in WWII, so Ralph and Alfred never served. Cornelius, Philip, and Bernard were drafted or enlisted. Anna Dietz proudly displayed a five-star flag in her window because she also had two sons-in-law in the service, my father, Roger Burdick, and Gertrude's husband, William Ferris. My father received an early medical discharge. He told his children it was because he had "flat feet". We discovered later on his discharge papers that actually he had a gastric ulcer.

My mother Eva, my brother John, my little sister Eva Jean, and I lived at the farm during the time Dad was in the Army. I spent the first half of second grade at the Catholic school in Kersey. Gertrude and Billy Ferris were also living there, at least some of the time. Anna Mae said that Billy did silly things to make her laugh.

The book. "Fox: Buffalo Swamp The History of Fox Township Pennsylvania", by Robert Schreiber Jr, available through Amazon, tells the story of Ku Klux Klan activity in Elk Co., opposed to foreigners and Catholics. The Pontzer family awoke one night to see a cross burning at a neighboring farm. That farm was Peter and Anna Dietz property. My mother, Eva, stated she saw the fire and her parents told her to stay in the house and let it burn. Anna later

68

befriended one of the instigators, who later attended Anna's funeral Mass, stating she would never go into a Catholic Church, except for Anna Dietz.

Barbara Langlotz

The other day, I was at the Cleveland Museum of Art for a one-hour docent tour focusing on war, because it was shortly after Memorial Day.

I saw an object which made me think of one of my and my kid's favorite activities on the farm, "dump diving"! It was a metal sculpture of an eagle from the early Roman times, about the size of a robin, which was mounted on the head of a weapon to lead men into battle. Who knew the Romans revered the eagle?

One of the objects I found in a dump was a smaller metal eagle, with about a 3" wingspan. It had been mounted on some small pole, probably a flagpole and hand carried. Uncle Alfred had told us where all the dumps were in the area, and since there was no trash pickup in the old days, we found lots of bottles and other objects. One item I found must have been just discarded; it was a paper license to sell oleomargarine in St Mary's, dated 1948. It had not been there long enough to be damaged by rain or dirt. I had it framed, and it is on my kitchen wall. Once, a repairman read it and asked, "Is that a joke?" No joke. The Dietz family churned their own butter so had no use for oleo, but I remember it was a white blob in a plastic bag with a little tablet of yellow dye that had to be kneaded into the white blob.

Anna Mae was only 4 years older than me, so when we were living at the farm during WWII, she was young enough to play with her young niece. She had a play area arranged in the attic with the usual girl toys, dolls, stuffed animals, tea sets, etc. We would go up there and play house, away from the busy life downstairs. Later in life, when I visited the farm, the attic door had a lock on it, and I missed going up to the quiet play area.

70

Farm women were tough! Grandma Dietz (Anna) had a garden where she grew vegetables and trees that bore fruit. She had chickens to feed and produce eggs and eventually become dinner. She had a churn to make butter, I know, I tried doing it. For some reason, I did not like the milk from the cows but insisted on milk from the store, but I did love the whipped cream Grandma made.

I remember one day in the back yard; Grandma was busy preparing the chickens for dinner. She would wring their necks, chop off their heads, hang them on the clothesline to drain the blood, and then pluck their feathers. I think the men butchered the cows and pigs. My mother, Eva, talked of eating blood sausage and beef heart; she served us beef heart at times but never blood sausage. All this while raising ten children, cleaning and laundering. I once asked my mother how her mother had dealt with babies in diapers. I was told Grandma would change the diaper and let the other clothing air dry. My mother told me that one day while Francie Gahr was out working, Helen went into labor. They had no phone, so she sent her kids out to play and delivered her own baby.

The Dietz kids were told not to go into the hay loft, but being kids, they went anyway and one of the girls stepped on a pitchfork and punctured her foot. They did not tell their mother. That girl was lucky not to get tetanus.

Cornelius (Nips) gave me a small seashell that he said he got while in the Philippines during the war. He also gave me some small wooden toys he had made. Bernie (Uncle Bunk) also gave me items made of wood; one is a small barrel with the name "Uncle Bunk" on it. He claimed to have gotten that name when a small child called him "Uncle Bunkle" and the name stuck.

Ernie Huff
Memories of the Farm

My family and I moved to 147 Dietz Road, "The Farm", in the summer of 2003 from our home in Toby (Fox Township) Pa. I was going into third grade at Fox Township Elementary school in Kersey PA. Our move was prompted by my uncle, John Parmigiani, selling the property to my mother Jane Huff (Parmigiani).

I recall going to the farm on numerous occasions prior to our move. My uncle owned the house but did not live there as he and my aunt, Ann Parmigiani (Paxton), were at the University of Michigan pursuing their PhDs. My mother was very passionate about the house and would frequently visit with my sister, Megan Thompson (Huff) and I to pick fresh fruit from the numerus trees and bushes on the property.

While the house was vacant, I recall having cookouts to celebrate summer holidays. These events would include my parents (Ed and Jane Huff), sister, grandmother Anna Mae Dietz (Parmigiani), grandfather Paul Parmigiani, aunt Sandy Blomgren (Parmigiani), first cousin Jennifer Melick (Blomgren), and relatives James Murnahan, Gregg Ferris, Bernadette Davis (Dietz), and James Davis.

I recall always sitting around the fire making hot dogs and eating picnic food. Grandpa Parmigani would always get the grill set up and Grandma would grill the burgers. Grandma would prepare the hamburgers ahead of time at her home, also in Kersey, and bring them out to grill. She would also bring craft singles to melt on top of the burgers.

As kids, Grandma would tell ghost stories to Megan, Jenny, and I. She would read books ahead of time to get ideas to share with us. One story she told was an army of undead people slowly marching across the field that looks beyond the barn near the fairgrounds. Megan, Jenny, and I were so scared, we didn't even want to walk up to the house!

During cookouts the group would usually go for a walk out to Joe's Camp, owned by Joe Luchini. Relatives would bring treats for Megan, Jenny and I and we would play with sparklers during the fourth of July holiday.

During my late grade school and middle school years, my friends and I would spend a lot of time at the house and biking around the neighborhood. Our group included Cole Pontzer, Phillip Pontzer, Brianna Cooney (Pontzer), Jarrod Lipsey, and Peter Cooney. We would play video games at my parents' house, play in the barns, and stay overnight at each other's homes.

It was a great place to be a kid. Looking back, I'm thankful we moved when we did. The relocation gave me a memorable, rewarding and adventurous childhood that I would have missed had we stayed in Toby. One memory that sticks out was playing in Alfred Dietz's barn that is visible from the back yard of the house. We would climb on hay bales, climb the rafters above the cows, and swing from ropes. My dad had a hunch of what we were doing but was never able to catch us. We were always able to hide in the loft when he came looking for us! Dad worked third shift and would come home around 6:20am. Sometimes we stayed up so late, we had to pretend we were sleeping when he got home!

As Megan and I got older, we started throwing our own parties at the house with friends from school. At times we would have groups of 20 plus kids. We would pitch tents and play yard games at night. We always enjoyed the vastness of the properly and the numerous places to hide outside when playing "kick the can". Even as I progressed through college years, the farm was always a place to come home to. I would invite college friends, girlfriends, and old friends from high school over to reminisce and enjoy each other's company. My mom loved when we had people over and always appreciated the layout of the house. She could spend time in another room as the house was big enough to not interfere with what we were doing.

I'm happy to have grown up and spend many formative years at the farm. Having moved back to Pennsylvania in 2022, I look forward to continuing traditions and continuing to be part of the family history that is 147 Dietz Road.

Reunion, 2025

2025 is 131 years removed from Anna Krellner first setting foot in America. 2025 is 121 years after the wedding of Peter and Anna Dietz.

Today, their descendants are small business owners, doctors, scientists, farmers, engineers, clergy, soldiers, journalists, teachers, and many other occupations. They are wives, husbands, parents, aunts, and uncles.

They reside in many if not all states, from Massachusetts to Oregon and California. From Florida to Alaska.

Some descendants have visited a very small town in Bavaria, others have spent a year or more as students in Germany. Others reside in Kersey, the site to which we return this July 26, 2025, to celebrate family.

The following poem is offered by a German woman residing in Louisville, whose book, "I Will Dance Again", I published in 2023. As far as I know, we are not related.

Antje Keller moved to the United States from Germany in 1957, which was the same year I was born.

Our Grandmother, Anna Krellner, moved to the United States from Germany as an eleven-year-old girl in the late 1800s.

I wonder if Anna had the same sense of wonder as expressed by Antje as she began her life in America.

Coming to America in October 1957
Antje Keller Simunac

Cloudless skies, a wide street stretching into the horizon.
On the left side, cars, cars and more cars lined up, ten or maybe fifty.
A car lot. BUY here, PAY HERE! What does it mean?
On the other side, ice cream, fifty cents, a banana split, a turtle sundae.
What does it mean?

Rows of wooden houses in street after street, grass plots behind, in front
and back no peas, carrots, apples or bushes of berries, just grass.
Those automobiles—huge, blue, green, red and white, some with fins.
Cool, just like the ones they showed in Life Magazine.

A store so large you could get lost in the aisles.
Meat, apples, milk, bread, cabbage, all in one store.
Nobody at home will believe it.
White bread with bologna for lunch. What is that?
Coffee from a jar, just add water and stir.
Where are the coffee beans?
America, the land of milk and honey.

Saddle shoes. What does that mean?
Montgomery Ward, a store where you can buy a coat, shoes, pretty
dresses, panties, a washing machine, vacuum cleaners.
And a plastic card to buy it all, pay ten dollars a month.

And it's cozy and warm in every room. Warm air comes from slats in the wall.
Heat even in the bedroom!
No need for a feather comforter. No schlepping coal.
And a bathtub with endless hot water. As much as you want!

Oh, and a box called TV in the living room where the family gathers to watch theatre.
Wagon Train, Bonanza, all about cowboys and Indians who live out west.
And they play a game called football, but not with their feet.
The players run, wrestle and fall down.
What does it mean?

And they bought a brand-new FORD FAIRLANE, light blue.
We drove it to Chicago, CHICAGO! I felt like a princess.

It was what they promised, in the magazines.
You can have it all, even if you are only eighteen and have no money.
Beautiful, exciting America.
They won't believe me at home.

www.ingramcontent.com/pod-product-compliance
Lightning Source LLC
Chambersburg PA
CBHW031524040426
42445CB00009B/385